The memories
and traditions of the

....

Family

started on

....

FAMILY ADVENT ACTIVITY BOOK

'TIS THE SEASON

Devotions, Recipes, and Memories
of the Christmas Season

Ink &
Willow

Contents

Why Celebrate Advent?—A Parent's Guide.....6

How to Use This Book 8

Family Advent Wreath 8

Waiting in Hope.....10

Games of Anticipation 14

Advent Ornaments 17

Advent Fun Facts 18

Holiday Cranberry Apple Bake 19

Living in Hope 20

Called to Faith.....22

Games of Blind Faith 26

Nativity Story 29

Nativity Fun Facts 30

Christmas Wine Cake 31

Living in Faith 32

Sudden and Unexpected Joy.....34

Gift Box Game 39

DIY Hot Chocolate Bar 42

St. Nicholas Fun Facts 44

Candy Cane Scones 45

Living in Joy 46

Spirit of Peace and Unity.....50

Peace and Goodwill to You 55

Decorating Tips for a Peaceful Christmas 57

Christmas Around the World Fun Facts 60

Christmas Morning Caramel Rolls 62

Living in Peace 64

Our Traditions.....66

Christmases Past.....72

References.....79

Why Celebrate Advent?

A Parent's Guide

The Lord is coming, always coming. When you have ears to hear and eyes to see, you will recognize him at any moment of your life. Life is Advent; life is recognizing the coming of the Lord. —HENRI J.M. NOUWEN

When we hear the word "advent" today, different images might come to mind—from candles on decorative wreaths to calendars concealing chocolates to the overall season of Christmas itself. Despite its history, however, the majority of believers in the Christian tradition mostly define Advent as the four-week (or forty-day) preparation period leading up to December 25, the date chosen by most church calendars as the day to recognize and celebrate the birth and incarnation of Jesus. While that may be part of what Advent is, it's not quite the full story.

The word *advent* is derived from the Latin *adventus* and the Greek *parousia*, which both signify a "coming." In the time of the early church, the practice of Advent began in a response to Jesus's command: "Therefore keep watch, because you do not know on what day your Lord will come" (Matthew 24:42). So the origin of Advent is less about Jesus coming to earth as a baby and more about preparing ourselves for his second coming.

As we read in the book of Acts, this "anticipation" began immediately after Jesus ascended to heaven. The disciples, staring upward and no doubt experiencing a range of emotions from confusion and sorrow to wonder and amazement, were confronted by two angelic beings, who asked, "Why do you stand here looking into the sky? This same Jesus, who has been taken from you into heaven, will come back in the same way you have seen him go into heaven" (Acts 1:11).

Today, Christians around the world still wait year-round in eager expectation for Jesus's return. Even so, since the Middle Ages, the actual season of Advent has become more connected to his first coming as a baby in Bethlehem. In the "new" definition, Advent references a time that extends from the end of November to December 25 and is specially marked by the four Sundays in between.

The themes for each of these Sundays vary slightly in different church traditions, but the most common are Hope, Faith, Joy, and Peace. Many churches mark each of these four Sundays by lighting a new candle in a wreath every week during the service. The actual origins of the wreath and candle tradition are a bit unclear since candles have long been symbols of hope and expectation through seasons of darkness. However, there is a story of a German Lutheran pastor in 1839 decorating a cart's wheel with an evergreen wreath and candles to provide a visual aid of counting down the days until Christmas for the children in his mission school. The evergreen, which remains a vibrant green even through the long and dark winter months, acts as a representation of God's unconditional love and his promise of eternal life. Red holly berries, which are often intertwined into the wreath, symbolize Jesus's blood and the crown of thorns. Depending on the country or the specific church tradition, between one and twenty-four candles may be lit during the four weeks leading up to Christmas. The most common tradition involves four candles—with one being lit each Sunday—and a fifth candle in the center marking Christmas Day and the celebration of Jesus's birth.

Though we may all have different ways of recognizing Jesus's first coming and anticipating his second, we as the people of God are all united in the practice of hope and expectation. In fact, it's a tradition that extends back almost to the Garden of Eden. Of course, the specific ways we observe this waiting have changed a lot over time.

Your church or family might have their own unique traditions during this season, and that is part of the beauty of Advent. However your family celebrates Advent, may you all experience a greater feeling of connection to one another as you draw nearer to Christ, reflect together on the importance of the season, create new traditions, and record memories throughout the many Christmases to come.

How to Use This Book

This book of memories and traditions was created with families in mind. And since all families are different, you'll find multiple options for customizing your family's experience, whether with the reflection questions, the application activities, or even the recipes. You know your family best, so feel free to adapt the content to what suits you!

While the format of this book has been created to follow the traditional rhythm of Advent—with enough readings and activities in each section to fill one week—the devotions and activities can be enjoyed in any order and even over the span of several Christmases. If there are any activities or pages you don't get to one year, feel free to leave them as "unopened gifts" you can enjoy the next year.

As your kids grow older, you can always return to this book year after year and get something new out of the activities and prompts. And the best part is that what you record in the Christmases Past section will quickly become a time capsule of memories shared with your favorite people during one of the most wondrous seasons of the year.

Family Advent Wreath

Perhaps your family already has an Advent tradition, but if not, try creating your own family wreath this season. Whether you use actual greenery or construct one with cloth or paper, make decorating it a family affair. Be sure to include four candles—one for hope, one for faith, one for joy, and one for peace—and a fifth one for the center.

Once the wreath is complete, place it on your kitchen table, on the hearth, near the front door, or in some other central area of your home. Then as your family reads the devotion each week, "light" each candle using a match, a bulb, a tea light, or colored paper (have adult supervision if using matches). When Christmas dawns, light the final fifth candle in the middle of the wreath. Throughout the season, may the wreath and the lit candles serve as a reminder of the promised Savior and his soon return.

Merry Christmas

WEEK ONE

Waiting
in Hope

O Come, O Come, Emmanuel

Read Luke 2:25–38

What better way to begin the season of anticipating Jesus's coming than with hope! Especially when we think about what it must have been like for the people of God who waited for Jesus's first coming. It probably felt like a long time for them. In fact, in the time between the close of Malachi at the end of the Old Testament and the opening of Matthew in the New, about four hundred years passed. Can you imagine waiting for something that long?

That "intertestamental" era is often called the period of silence, because no one was sharing any great words of prophecy or comfort, and God seemed to have gone "radio silent." No letters, phone calls, or messages from heaven. It was bad enough that Malachi's last word in his book was *destruction*. But then God's people went through four centuries of terrible darkness and violence, marked by captivity, oppression, war, and persecution. Talk about a cliff-hanger! What do you think it would have been like to wait your whole life for something good to happen after everything you knew fell apart? Do you think you would have been able to keep hoping?

What do you think it would have been like to wait your whole life for something good to happen after everything you knew fell apart?

We may not be living in a time of religious persecution, desperate poverty, or life-threatening oppression like so many faced back then, but life now is still far from perfect. We've all experienced a lot of bad stuff, like wars, hate, sickness, bullying, fear, loneliness, loss, and paralyzing hopelessness that often keep us from believing God is really there. But that's the beauty of who God is and how he acts. He always shows up in the most remarkable ways, at the most unexpected times, right when all hope seems lost. He did it with a tiny baby born in a dark stable in an unimportant town out in the middle of nowhere, and he's doing the same thing today, though it may look a little different.

* * *

If you think about it, God showing up after we've had to wait makes the moment hoped for even more miraculous and wonderful—like a beautiful sunrise after a long, dark night or a fun trip after the school term or a much-anticipated birthday after weeks of counting down the days. The anticipation for something isn't always fun, but sometimes it can be exciting, and it almost always makes the gift or miracle or event even sweeter when it finally arrives.

But what about when waiting doesn't have the happy ending we wanted? In retrospect, those instances can make the waiting feel like it wasn't worth it. But as believers, we should hold on to a kind of "confident hope" that our faith in God's promises will one day be fulfilled in his eternal kingdom. As 2 Corinthians 1:20 says, "For no matter how many promises God has made, they are 'Yes' in Christ. And so through him the 'Amen' is spoken by us to the glory of God." This "Amen" is something we claim in hope, even when we don't know the outcome. For if we knew exactly when and how God was going to show up, we wouldn't have to have faith, and we wouldn't be able to practice trusting him.

It's funny, but when we hear the word "wait" today, we usually take it to mean "stop" or "sit still." But that is not quite the way God intended us to wait. The Hebrew word for hope *(tikvah)* contains the root *kavah,* which means "to wait." In other words, waiting is one of the main parts of hoping. But as we see in the lives of so many biblical figures and people throughout history, waiting doesn't mean stopping or hanging around

God always shows up in the most remarkable ways, at the most unexpected times, right when all hope seems lost.

until something happens. Abraham had to wait twenty-five years after hearing he would have a son before Isaac was born, but in that time, he had to leave his homeland to fulfill God's promise. The Israelites had to wait forty years before they reached the Promised Land, but they never would have arrived there at all if they had decided to wait around in Egypt. Anna and Simeon waited their entire lives to see the promised Messiah, but while they waited, they kept showing up in the temple to worship and pray. All these stories show people living out their faith, even amid long waiting seasons.

God has called all of us to do the same thing today—to wait on his timing, but to keep moving forward, to keep trusting, to keep loving and serving others, and to keep seeking God even while we wait (Psalm 27:14; Luke 12:35–40; Romans 12:12; James 5:7–8). Obviously, waiting on the Lord isn't for the faint of heart. What a relief it is to know we have the Spirit who helps us when we feel like giving up!

Reflection Questions

- What is the longest time you waited for something?

- When have you become impatient in a season of waiting and tried to speed things up in your own way? What happened?

- What do you feel like you are waiting for right now?

Family Prayer for Hope

Heavenly Father, you know we're not very good at waiting and that we like to be in control. Help us to practice the positive side of waiting by putting our hope in you, for you are our help and our shield, our ever-present Comforter whose promises are good and trustworthy. Teach us how to hope for the small, everyday things we are longing for today, in the same way as we hope for your return someday soon. In Jesus's name, amen.

Family Advent Wreath (see page 8): Light the Hope candle.

Practicing Hope

This week, have each member of the family choose one of the following activities to practice hope (pick one that is age appropriate!):

- Instead of keeping it to yourself, share a hope you've been thinking about with someone you trust.

- At the breakfast or dinner table, talk about one thing you're excited about or looking forward to that day.

- Read Psalm 33 every morning.

- Read Psalm 27 every night before bed.

- Memorize Psalm 42:11, Isaiah 40:31, Romans 5:1–4, or Romans 8:24–25.

- Take time to read through the book of Micah.

- Read one chapter from 1 Thessalonians each day and journal your reflections.

Games of Anticipation

◆

Have you ever skipped to the end (or at least thought
about doing so) of a book or movie because you were
dying to see how everything turned out? Sometimes the
anticipation is more exciting than the actual resolution,
but a great story builds high-stakes anticipation while
also delivering the perfectly unexpected conclusion.
Keep that in mind as you dive into the following games.

Who Am I?

For 4 or more players

Ages 4+

What you'll need:

1 sheet of paper for each player

1 drawing utensil for each player

How to Play

1. With the sheet of paper in portrait orientation, fold it in half so that the top edge lines up with the bottom edge. Fold one more time the same way so that the piece of paper ends up with three creased lines.

2. Using the creases as guidelines, draw the head of a person, creature, monster, or mythical being in the top space. Feel free to add a background if desired. Extend the neck down just slightly into the second space. Don't show the others your drawing!

3. Fold the paper so that the head is hidden and pass the paper to the left.

4. With your new piece of paper (only the small neck lines should be showing), draw a torso for the person, creature, monster, or mythical being. Extend the torso just slightly down into the third space.

5. Fold the paper so that the head as well as the torso are hidden and again pass the paper to the left.

6. Using only the vague guidelines of the torso, draw the hips and legs in the third space. Extend the ankles slightly into the last space, fold the paper down, and pass one more time to the left.

7. In the last space, draw the feet.

8. Unfold the papers to reveal what people or creatures have been created!

What Happens Next?

For 4 or more players

Ages 8+

What you'll need:

1 sheet of paper for each player

1 drawing utensil for each player

How to Play

1. Have every player come up with an opening line for a story and write it at the top of their sheet of paper. (Optional: mark your paper with your initials or a tiny symbol in the bottom right corner of the page so that you recognize it when it comes back to you.)

2. Pass all papers one person to the left.

3. Using the line at the top of the new piece of paper, write down what happens next in the story. Then fold the top of the paper down so that it covers the first line and pass the paper to the left again.

4. Using the visible sentence or phrase on the new piece of paper, draw a picture to illustrate what happens next. Then accordion fold the already folded top of the paper so that the first line remains hidden and the second one becomes covered. With only the illustration showing, pass the paper one person to the left again.

5. Using only the illustration on the new piece of paper as a guide, write a sentence describing what happens next.

6. Continue passing the pattern around the circle until the stories are back with their original authors.

7. Unfold the papers and take turns reading aloud the stories created.

Advent Ornaments

As you begin to pull out ornaments for the Christmas tree, set aside twenty-four special ones and wrap them or place them in festive bags or boxes. Each day during Advent, take turns opening up one wrapped ornament and hanging it on the tree.

When you take down the tree at the end of the season, feel free to prewrap those special ornaments so you can continue the tradition next year!

Advent
Fun Facts

Similar to Lent, Advent began as a season of fasting and prayer for Christians around the world.

The most popular colors for Advent candles are violet and rose, but some churches use blue candles or red ones. In the traditional pattern, the violet candles, which are typically used for the first, second, and fourth Sundays, represent prayer, sacrifice, and reflection. The rose candle, which is lit on the third Sunday, represents rejoicing. Sometimes a white candle is placed in the center of the wreath to symbolize the celebration of Jesus's birth.

On the third Sunday of Advent, a special pink or rose candle is lit to signify the joy that the time of fasting and penitence is more than halfway over. This is called *Gaudete* Sunday, which means "joy" in Latin.

Recipe

Holiday Cranberry Apple Bake

Serves 6 to 8

Ingredients

Butter for greasing the baking dish

FRUIT LAYER

3 cups chopped apple (any kind works, but pink or red are more festive!)

2 cups cranberries, washed and rinsed

2 tablespoons all-purpose flour/almond flour/gluten-free flour/ etc.

1 cup granulated sugar (or ¾ cup honey, ¾ cup maple syrup, ⅔ cup agave, or 1 teaspoon stevia)

TOPPING

3 cups oats

¾ cup pecans, chopped (or ⅓ cup rice cereal or ½ cup pumpkin seeds)

½ cup all-purpose flour (or almond flour or gluten-free flour)

½ cup brown sugar (or ½ cup coconut sugar or ½ cup date sugar)

½ cup melted unsalted butter (or ½ cup applesauce, ½ cup Greek yogurt, ½ cup ghee, or ½ cup coconut oil)

Directions

- Preheat the oven to 350°F. Grease a 9x13-inch glass or metal baking dish.

- In a plastic bag or mixing bowl, mix the fruit layer ingredients until the fruit pieces are well coated. Layer the fruit evenly into the greased baking dish.

- In a small bowl, combine all the ingredients in the topping layer until it has a crumbly texture. Spread the oat topping evenly over the fruit layer.

- Bake at 350°F for 45 minutes, or until the topping is browned and the apple filling is bubbling.

- Enjoy with cream for breakfast, dessert, or a tasty snack!

Living in Hope

Hope for You

Staying hopeful can be hard when you feel like none of your prayers are being answered or as if God isn't even there. When that happens, try to remember specific ways God has shown up for you in the past or specific prayers that were answered. Write them down so you can turn to them whenever you feel hopeless. You can also list things you are thankful for as a way of turning your focus away from what you don't have and toward what you do have.

Hope for Your Family

Keeping up a spirit of hopefulness is much easier when we know we're not alone, which is why families are such wonderful gifts! Be sure to practice hope together by really listening to one another's prayers, wishes, and dreams and supporting them when you can. And when a hope or dream seems impossible, come together in prayer, remembering that every good and perfect gift comes from God, our loving Father and Bringer of Light.

Hope for Your Community

In a world that often feels full of darkness or sadness, experiencing even small moments of beauty or comfort can encourage us to be more hopeful. How can your family bring hope to others by sharing beauty and comfort? Here are some ideas:

- Fill small bags or holiday stockings with treats, hygiene essentials, or other gifts and keep them in your car to hand out when you see someone in need.

- When you're in a drive-thru line, pay for the order of the person behind you.

- Help a neighbor decorate their house.

- Invite someone who doesn't have family nearby to spend Christmas with you.

WEEK TWO

Called to Faith

O Come, All Ye Faithful

Read Luke 1:26–38

Can you imagine having an angel show up in your room and say you were going to become the mom of the Son of God? Well, that's exactly what happened to Mary—and she was only a teenager! After hearing that incredible promise from the angel of the Lord, Mary displayed incredible faith with the simple answer of "I am the Lord's servant. . . . May your word to me be fulfilled" (verse 38).

Joseph, Jesus's chosen earthly dad, also showed an amazing kind of faith when an angel appeared to *him* in a dream, and told him that not only should he go ahead and take Mary as his wife, but that the son she was going to have would be the coming Messiah. Dreams can be kind of hard to believe sometimes, but Joseph didn't let that stop him. Matthew 1:24 tells us, "When Joseph woke up, he did what the angel of the Lord had commanded him and took Mary home as his wife." Signed, sealed, no questions asked.

The story of Jesus's birth is surrounded by stories of the faithful God called. And while not many of us have angels popping into our houses or dreams, God is still calling us to great faith today. Though centuries after Joseph, Mary, and the birth of Jesus, Christmas is a great time for remembering the calling placed on us and for finding encouragement in our own faith journeys. Christmas reminds us of all the blessings that come from putting our faith in God. During this Advent season, we can put our faith in God's promises. We can have faith that families will be restored, that the Holy Spirit will reach family and friends we've been praying for, and that his goodness will continue past December 25.

God is still calling us to great faith today.

* * *

What does the Bible say about faith? Hebrews 11:1 tells us that "Faith is confidence in what we hope for and assurance about what we do not see." Though we won't "confidently" know every answer this side of heaven, we can always trust in God's Word and his power. When we put our faith in God, we are saying we trust him completely. And putting our trust and faith in God is the best place to be, since he has the big and little things under control and cares about all of them. As Matthew 6:26–27 reminds us,

"Look at the birds of the air; they do not sow or reap or store away in barns, and yet your heavenly Father feeds them. Are you not much more valuable than they? Can any one of you by worrying add a single hour to your life?"

Of course, replacing worry with faith won't magically fix all of our problems, but it will teach us how to focus on what is more important. And the good news is, faith isn't only a gift at Christmas, but all year round! It's not like presents, or Christmas trees, or our favorite Christmas songs that we sing in December. Instead, faith is a *promise* of Christmas that rings true every day.

Many people call Christmas a season of miracles, and it is (though maybe not in the "I'm hoping for the miracle of a unicorn or some other expensive gift under the tree" kind of way). Instead, Christmas is a season when we can celebrate the miracle proclaimed by angels in Luke 2:11: "Today in the town of David a Savior has been born to you; he is the Messiah, the Lord." We can also give thanks for the miracles in our own lives, whether they're *for* us like the one for blind Bartimaeus, who was healed because of his faith (Mark 10:46–52), or *through* us like the one given to all of Egypt because of Joseph's faithfulness (Genesis 37–45). Even if the miracle you pray for doesn't get answered in the way you hoped, have faith that God is still working, and that he is still trustworthy and good.

Faith is confidence in what we hope for and assurance about what we do not see.

Ultimately, the greatest gift is that we can place our faith in the same God who speaks to us through angels and his Word, who created the heavens and the earth, who sent his son Jesus so that we might be free, and who loves each one of us more than we could ever ask or imagine!

Reflection Questions

- Who is someone you trust? Why do you trust them?

- Think of a time when you struggled to stay strong in your faith. What helped you get out of that funk?

- What are you praying for in faith right now?

Family Prayer for Faith

Dear God, we are not always the best at holding on to our faith and trusting you in all things. During this Christmas season, may your Holy Spirit remind us of your goodness and your promises, so that we can celebrate and honor you this season. May our faith, no matter how small, shine a light to others and point our family and friends to you. In Jesus's name, amen.

Family Advent Wreath (see page 8): Light the Faith candle.

Practicing Faith

This week, have each member of the family choose one of the following activities to practice faith (select one that is age appropriate!).

- Pray for everyone in your family before bed each night.

- Pick a specific time of day (like when you're brushing your teeth, riding in the car, or about to turn on the TV) and say a short prayer of thankfulness.

- Memorize Ephesians 2:8–9, Proverbs 3:5–6, or James 1:2–4.

- Look up a country where Christians are being persecuted for their faith and make a habit of praying for the people there every day this week.

- Read Hebrews 11.

- Research the life of a missionary or martyr.

- Share your personal story of faith with someone new.

Games of Blind Faith

---◆---

How well do you trust the members of your family?
Enough for a trust fall, or not quite as far as you
could throw a Christmas tree? Though neither of
those options is being suggested, the following
activities might require you to have at least a little
faith in those around you.

Blind Drawing

For 2 or more players

Ages 4+

What you'll need:

8½ x 11-inch white or color paper and drawing utensils

How to Play

1. Choose one person to be the head elf. Everyone else is a workshop elf.

2. Set up the workshop elves with paper and pencils and have them close their eyes.

3. Have the head elf give directions on what to draw. It could be a Christmas tree with presents, a snowman, Santa's workshop, a fireplace, a winter scene, or anything else the head elf decides.

4. Keeping their eyes closed, the workshop elves must try to draw the images as best they can. (Suggestion: it's easier if they keep their pencils on the paper at all times.)

5. Once the picture is complete, have everyone open their eyes and share the results. You can either tally points for accuracy or creativity, or just see whose is the funniest!

In the Manner of the Word

For 3 or more players

Ages 6+

What you'll need:

Nothing!

How to Play

1. Choose one person to be the first guesser. While that person covers their ears or leaves the room, the other players choose an adverb (descriptive word ending in -ly, such as *carefully, quickly,* or *joyfully*). Once everyone agrees on the word and what it means, bring the guesser back into the room.

2. To guess the chosen word, the guesser will begin to ask the other players to perform certain actions in the manner of the word. (For example: "Dad, pick up that book in the manner of the word." Or: "Susan and Sophia, give each other a high

   five in the manner of the word.") The players respond by completing those actions in a way that shows the agreed-upon adverb.

3. As the players continue carrying out the guesser's directions, the guesser can call out adverbs until the right one is revealed.

4. Choose a new guesser for the next round. Though this game does not need to be played competitively, you can keep score by tallying up how many actions are completed before the guesser gets the right answer.

Nativity Story

If you have a nonbreakable nativity scene—or aspiring thespians in your house—try an interactive twist on reading the nativity story by inviting your kids to take an active role in it. While someone reads the story, let your child(ren) move the nativity figures along with what is happening. This way of experiencing the story can be especially helpful for kids who might struggle with listening or sitting still.

If you don't have a nativity scene or if your kids like acting, let them try acting out the story as someone narrates.

The Nativity

Fun Facts

St. Francis of Assisi, an Italian friar, was the first person to create a nativity scene with live animals.[1]

Mary and Joseph had to travel about ninety miles to reach Bethlehem from Nazareth. On foot, the journey would have taken about four days to a week.

The reason we celebrate Christmas on December 25 is because Emperor Constantine decided in AD 336 to align the holiday with the winter solstice. As for Jesus's actual birth, it's more likely that it took place in the spring, since that was the usual time of year for shepherds to be out with their flocks.[2]

Although nativities today usually depict baby Jesus in a wooden manger, it is more likely that he was placed in a stone feeding trough.[3]

It's highly possible that both Joseph and Jesus were stonemasons or builders instead of carpenters, since the Greek word used to describe their profession is *tektōn*, which means "craftsman." Since the majority of structures in the first century were built out of stone, it's likely that is the material they worked with.[4]

Recipe

Christmas Wine Cake

Makes one 10-inch cake

Ingredients

Butter or baking spray, for greasing

Yellow cake mix (Duncan Hines is the best, but feel free to use your favorite!)

¾ cup sherry cooking wine

¾ cup vegetable oil

Jell-O instant vanilla pudding mix (3.4-ounce size)

4 eggs

Dusting of powdered sugar

Directions

- Preheat the oven to 350°F. Grease a 10-inch Bundt pan.

- Put the cake mix, sherry, oil, pudding mix, and eggs in a large bowl and combine using a hand mixer for about 4 minutes, until blended well. Pour the batter into the greased Bundt pan.

- Bake for 35 to 45 minutes, until a toothpick inserted in the center comes out clean. (For high altitude, check for doneness at 25 minutes.)

- Remove from the oven and let the cake cool for a couple minutes before turning it onto a serving plate. After completely cool, dust with powdered sugar.

- Enjoy!

Living in Faith

Faith for You

Whether you're feeling like you can't get out of a slump or you're hoping to deepen your faith, one way you can do that is by going straight to God's Word. Write out what you are struggling with (for example: worry or fear or anger) and then look up a verse that reminds you of God's promise (like John 14:27). Remember, God's Word never comes back empty!

Faith for Your Family

God uses the people close to us to encourage us in our faith and lives. Even when you don't have all the answers, you can still pray for everyone in your family and encourage them to keep up practices of faith, like going to church, reading the Bible, and taking part in worship. You can also be open about what you are dealing with and about what doubts and fears you might be facing, because sometimes we can find encouragement in knowing we are not struggling alone. This week, spend some time over a meal together and share words of encouragement, lessons you're learning, or challenges you might be facing.

Faith for Your Community

The prayers of believers are powerful. This week spend some time faithfully praying for your local community (maybe look up businesses, ministries, or churches nearby) and for communities around the world (pull up a world map and pray for a different country each night).

WEEK THREE

Sudden and
Unexpected
Joy

Joy to the World

Read Matthew 2:1–12

Have you ever had a bad day that changed suddenly into one of the best days ever when something fun, exciting, or surprising happened? Maybe it was a terrible school or workday when nothing was going right, you messed up, the weather was awful, or you were feeling left out or sick, and then—unexpectedly—you aced that test, were given an unbelievable opportunity, or received a surprise gift or the exact good news you had been hoping for. Whatever it was, in that moment, you experienced the most wonderful turn—going from the worst of the worst to the best of the best when you least expected it. It's the same kind of thing that happens in most books and movies right near the end. Everything is going wrong, the characters appear to be trapped in the dark with no way out, and the chance of a happy ending seems to be impossible. And then, right when all hope feels lost, something amazing and even miraculous happens. The hero finds a secret weapon, the good guys band together in a way they've never done before, and against all odds they win the day.

Strangely enough, there wasn't a word that existed in the English language to describe this kind of happy reversal from bad to great, so J. R. R. Tolkien (the guy who wrote *The Hobbit* and *The Lord of the Rings*) came up with one. He thought a helpful way to describe it was the opposite of a catastrophe. You know what a catastrophe is, right? When everything goes horribly wrong all at once? Think of a lion escaping its enclosure at the zoo or your parents coming home right when you and your siblings or friends have destroyed the house. Pretty bad, right? Now imagine the opposite, and you get what Mr. Tolkien called a *eucatastrophe*. That *eu* prefix that precedes *cat* in *catastrophe* is from the Greek root *eu*, which means "good," "well," or "joy." It's the same prefix that's used in words like *eucalyptus* (a healthy plant) and *Eucharist* (another name for the Lord's Supper). By adding those two little letters to *catastrophe*, Mr. Tolkien created a new word that could describe the unexpected and miraculous turn of joy when all seems hopeless.

> *And then, right when all hope feels lost, something amazing and even miraculous happens.*

Even though Tolkien didn't come up with his fancy new word until 1947, the idea of eucatastrophe has been around for a long time. In fact, you could say Jesus was the original eucatastrophe-bringer (eucatastropher?): first when he came to earth, and again when he gave himself up to die on a cross for everyone in the world.

If you remember from the first devotional, things were pretty bad in the world—and in Israel especially—when the angel Gabriel showed up to tell Mary that she would give birth to the Son of God. The Roman Empire was in charge and had inflicted some rather severe restrictions and laws on most of what is now Europe and parts of the Middle East. The Jews were being persecuted (or mistreated) for their faith, heavy taxes were forcing many people into poverty, and fighting was becoming very common. And then, right in the middle of all that hard stuff, all that mess, God stepped in, arriving in human form the same way the rest of us did—as a tiny, helpless baby.

Thankfully, there are no "unimportant" roles in God's eyes. We are all precious in his sight, and he has specific plans and callings for each of us.

The shepherds on the hillside outside Bethlehem must have felt powerless against all that was going on in their worlds. After all, they were just shepherds. Have you ever felt like you were "just" something? Just a kid, just a student, just a stay-at-home parent, just an assistant, just a_____? Thankfully, there are no "unimportant" roles in God's eyes. We are all precious in his sight, and he has specific plans and callings for each of us (Jeremiah 29:11; Psalm 139; Isaiah 43:1–2). In fact, in another kind of eucatastrophe, God called the shepherds to be the first to hear about Jesus's arrival—from a chorus of heavenly angels, no less. That had to be an incredible (and terrifying) sight. And talk about a complete reversal from fear to joy, from bad to good, and from powerless to purpose-filled!

Much farther away, a group of magi (wise priests from Persia) saw a star that would eventually lead them to Jesus. Matthew 2:10 says, "When they saw the star, they were overjoyed." Clearly, there was a lot of joy going around, and all because of the eucatastrophic intervention of God. Thanks to his perfect planning, a bunch of shepherd "nobodies" became the first outsiders to see the Savior of the world and the first people called to share the Good News of his coming. And thanks to God's protective providence, some wise guys from far away were able to deliver gifts to Jesus that prophesied the eucatastrophe of his sacrifice on a cross and of his coming kingdom.

Reflection Questions

- How do you think you would have felt if you were one of the shepherds or the magi?

- What's one of the best surprises or gifts you've ever experienced? How did it make you feel?

- How do you think God has called you to bring a "eucatastrophe" to those around you?

Family Prayer for Joy

Dear God, thank you so much for the gift of your Son, Jesus, the best and most perfect gift any of us will ever receive. Thank you for saving us not from far away but by coming down into the mess and pain of this world and becoming a human like us. Thank you for the beauty of joy and for the way you bring eucatastrophes into our lives every day. Help us to reflect your joy back to our friends, family, neighbors, and others you have placed around us. Teach us how to see the kind of joy the magi felt even when things are hard. Give us courage to be like the shepherds and continue to share the Good News of salvation to everyone we meet. Fill us with your joy this season. In Jesus's name, amen.

Family Advent Wreath (see page 8): Light the Joy candle.

(continued on next page)

Practicing Joy

This week, have each member of the family choose one of the following activities to practice joy (pick one that is age appropriate!):

- Say thank you or good morning to a different person every day this week.

- Think of five things you're thankful for or excited about before bed each night.

- Read through the letter to the Philippians.

- Memorize Psalm 100.

- Find an example of a eucatastrophe in a book or movie.

- Memorize Luke 2:8–20.

- Think of a unique way you can bring someone else joy this week and then do it.

- Share the Good News by explaining the real meaning of Christmas to someone.

Games of Great Joy

◆

With family gatherings, movie nights, snowball fights,
and cookie decorating, Christmas can be such a fun
season. However your family chooses to celebrate, may
these activities (yes, the DIY hot chocolate bar isn't
exactly a "game") bring you lots of joy and laughter!

Gift Box

What you'll need:

For 4 or more players

Ages 8+

strips or squares
of paper for every
player

pens or pencils

empty gift box

timer

How to Play

1. Give every player at least two pieces of paper (or more if you prefer a longer game) and have everyone write down one word or short phrase on each piece. The word can be a person, place, or thing, but it should be something everyone would know. For a festive game, encourage everyone to write down Christmas-themed words.

2. Collect all the pieces of paper in the gift box and mix them up.

3. Arrange the players in a circle and number off into two teams so that players from the same team aren't sitting next to each other.

4. Choose a player to go first and give that person the gift box. With 30 seconds on the timer, that player should describe one word at a time from the box without saying that specific word or using rhymes. The player's teammates should try to guess the word as quickly as possible. The player with the box can go through as many words as possible before the timer runs out.

5. Continue to pass the gift box around the circle, alternating teams, until all the words have been guessed correctly.

6. Have each team gather the words they guessed and correctly tally them up.

7. Put the pieces of paper back in the gift box. The second round begins where round one ended. If the player who ended round one still had time left on the clock, that player will begin round two with what time was remaining. If the time ran out, round two begins with the next person in the circle.

8. In round two, instead of describing the word, the player with the gift box can say only one word as a hint to the other players (remember what was said in round one!).

9. Continue play until the gift box is again empty, then count up the points for each team.

10. Put the pieces of paper back in the gift box. In round three, the player with the gift box can use only charades to describe the word on each piece of paper. If needed, allow 45 seconds or even a minute per player for this round.

11. In the final round, the player with the gift box can use only sounds to describe the word on each paper.

12. At the end of the game, add up the points for each round to see which team wins!

DIY
Hot Chocolate Bar

What better way to spread joy than with a personalized cocoa bar, complete with marshmallows, cookies for dipping, chocolate truffles, and special mugs? Set up your own hot chocolate bar for a fun impromptu night with the family, or plan ahead and invite some of your friends or neighbors. The joy of this delicious activity is that it can be as simple or as fancy as you want it to be and will certainly be a hit either way! (It's hard to go wrong when chocolate is involved.)

Hot Chocolate Topping Options

- Flavored syrups (mint, raspberry, orange, coffee, huckleberry, vanilla, etc.)

- Marshmallows (mini, jumbo, regular, or crème)

- Whipped cream

- Candy (crushed or broken into pieces)

- Cookies or graham crackers for dipping

- Salted caramel

- Sea salt

- Chocolate truffles

- Candy canes, chocolate spoons, or cinnamon sticks for stirring

- Espresso shot

- Coffee creamer, whipping cream, or milk of your choice

- Sprinkles

- Cinnamon or cocoa powder for sprinkling on top

- Any other toppings you'd like!

St. Nicholas

Fun Facts

 Santa Claus is actually based on a real figure from the third century known as St. Nicholas. Born in what is now modern-day Turkey, he spent much of his childhood giving gifts to the poor and performing other acts of charity. He eventually became a bishop.[5]

 The Dutch name for St. Nicholas is *Sinterklaas*, which is how we got the name "Santa Claus."

 The name *Nicholas* means "the people's victory" in Greek.

 During the Middle Ages, a group of French nuns secretly delivered food and other gifts to the poor. They credited St. Nicholas as the giver, which led to the tradition of him being behind all anonymous gift-giving at Christmas.[6]

Recipe

Candy Cane Scones

Makes 12 to 15 scones

Ingredients

2 cups all-purpose flour or gluten-free flour

3 tablespoons granulated sugar (or 3 tablespoons coconut sugar, 2 tablespoons honey, or 2 tablespoons maple syrup)

1½ teaspoons baking powder

½ teaspoon salt

5 tablespoons chilled unsalted butter

½ cup whipping cream

¼ teaspoon vanilla extract

1 large egg

Crushed candy canes (small pieces are better!), white chocolate chips, or any other toppings you like!

Egg white or milk, for glazing

Directions

- Preheat the oven to 425°F. Line a baking sheet with parchment paper (especially if using candy canes).

- In a small bowl, mix the flour, sugar, baking powder, and salt. Grate in the chilled butter.

- In a separate bowl, mix the cream, vanilla, and egg.

- Form a well in the dry ingredients and pour in the wet mixture. Mix thoroughly with a wooden spoon. Fold in crushed candy cane pieces, white chocolate chips, or any other filling of your choice.

- Form 12 to 15 round, 1-inch-thick scones by rolling into balls. Place on the prepared baking sheet, then flatten the top and base. Brush the tops with egg white or milk.

- Bake for 15 to 17 minutes or until lightly brown. Let cool.

- Enjoy with Devonshire cream and Christmas tea!

Living in Joy

Joy for You

Regardless of what you may think about self-care, taking time to do things that bring you joy is a vital part of growing in emotional and spiritual maturity. After all, you can't give joy to others if you rarely experience it yourself. Even God took the time to enjoy his work after each day of creation. So, what are the activities that bring you joy? Who are the people who always manage to fill you up when you feel you're running on empty? When are you at your happiest? Is it when you're with others or taking some time alone? When you're shopping or sitting with a book by the fire? When you're hosting a holiday tea or just baking cookies with the kids? Find time this week to do one thing that brings you joy.

Joy for Your Family

The law of returns states that whenever you give or sacrifice something, you usually receive a greater return. The gift of joy is no exception. When you bring joy to others, you experience an overwhelming sense of joy yourself. In a way, joy acts like a snowball rolling down a hill, picking up momentum and increasing in strength the longer it lasts. With that in mind, how can you start a joyful "chain reaction" in your family? Maybe by surprising someone with cookies or breakfast in bed, or by orchestrating Secret Santa gifts or acts of service in the days leading up to Christmas. Whatever you do, remember to do it with a joyful attitude!

Joy for Your Community

Christmas is often considered to be one of the most joy-filled times of year, but unfortunately, that isn't always true for everyone. As believers, we are called to be joy-givers and light-bringers—certainly throughout the year, but maybe especially at Christmas. Your family may already have some traditions for sharing joy with others, but if you need a few more ideas, check out the list on the next page!

Participate in a toy drive.

Treat another family to a Christmas dinner.

Buy another family a tree.

Write a letter or send a care package to someone in the armed forces.

Volunteer in a soup kitchen, shelter, or other missionary organization.

Organize a neighborhood cookie exchange.

Donate clothes, toys, or other household items.

Host a gift exchange or Christmas party for kids and give their parents a night off.

WEEK FOUR

Spirit of Peace
and Unity

PEACE

Silent Night

Read Luke 2:1–20

The Christmas season is always one of the busiest times of year. From decorating our houses and baking tasty treats to performing in pageants and attending parties—and let's not forget the gift buying, wrapping, and giving—the "most wonderful time of the year" is definitely one of the most chaotic times of the year. No matter what the hymn says, all is *not* calm, and finding moments of peace can sometimes feel impossible.

But do you know what? If we had been present during the first-ever Christmas events more than two thousand years ago, we probably would have also struggled to find peaceful moments. Think about how stressful it probably was: Joseph and Mary had to travel from Nazareth to Bethlehem—a journey that would have taken anywhere from four days to a full week. They would have also had to navigate through nightmare traffic since the whole Roman Empire had been commanded to return to their hometowns for the census (basically a time when the ruling authorities counted people for tax reasons, so this was definitely not a "vacation" type of trip). On top of all that, Mary was nine months pregnant (all the mamas will know how uncomfortable, tired, and perhaps even a bit cranky she would have been feeling)!

> *The word for* peace *is* shalom, *which basically means "being whole."*

When Mary and Joseph finally reached their destination, their hopes probably on a hot bath or at least a comfy bed, they found out that none of the inns had any rooms left. Their only option was a stable, which came with all kinds of neighing, braying, clucking, and mooing from the animals that surrounded them. And let's not forget the host of angels who triumphantly (aka LOUDLY) declared Jesus's birth to the shepherds. As if that wasn't chaotic enough, then the shepherds arrived. In fact, they not only rushed into the stable (adding to the number of bodies, animals, and noise in the space) but also went about declaring they had met baby Jesus to everyone who would listen (Luke 2:17–18). In other words, the night Jesus was born was definitely *not* calm or silent. Far from what we would describe as peaceful.

If we used an English dictionary's definition of *peace*, we might feel confused about how anyone could expect "calm," "order," and "tranquility" during the holidays. But in the Old Testament, the word for *peace* is *shalom*, which basically means "being whole."

In fact, the word describes the blessing of being a part of God's covenant community. In the New Testament, the Greek *eirēnē* (i-raynay) is used for *peace*, and it also refers to the "oneness" we have when we are joined together with God and one another through Christ. For a Christian, peace is much more than silence or calmness; it's the gift of being unified and made complete through our relationship with God. And this is a gift we wouldn't have access to without the birth of Jesus.

* * *

Before Jesus was born, only a select group of people were covered under the covenant that promised peace. But because of his birth, *everyone* gained access to peace with God (Romans 5:1; 1 Thessalonians 5:9). And because of his death on the cross, we no longer have to be separated from God and instead can have a personal relationship with him. No wonder the angels sang and the shepherds spread the news to all they met!

The fact that Jesus's birth allows us to be at peace, or be united, with God is a reason to rejoice, but it should also create a deep sense of rest in our souls. When the hustle and bustle and general chaos of the Christmas season threaten to overwhelm you, remember that the peace of God is different from the world's peace. Remember that Jesus is our Prince of Peace and that he promises to see us through all things (Colossians 3:15; Philippians 4:7; John 16:33). With the truths spelled out in these verses, allow yourself to experience the real peace the season offers as you recognize your security in Christ.

> *No wonder the angels sang and the shepherds spread the news to all they met!*

Have you ever heard of the Christmas Truce of 1914? It's definitely one of the most incredible examples of peace and "oneness" in action at Christmas. As a quick summary, the year 1914 was only the beginning of World War I, which would end up claiming more than twenty million lives. However, that Christmas, British, French, Austrian, German, and Russian soldiers from all along what was called the Western Front put down their weapons and instead extended the hand of peace. Many soldiers even crossed the no-man's-land and exchanged rations and played games together. Through their example, we can see that Christmas is a season that not only encourages us to find peace but also reminds us to be at peace with others. It is generally a time where strife and discord tend to cease.

But again, peace goes deeper than a lack of disruption or tension with those around us. Because Jesus was born, we can now join a great family of believers around the world who also choose to trust in his name for salvation (2 Corinthians 13:11; Ephesians 4:2–7). As the Church, we are called to be instruments of God's peace to the rest of the world (Matthew 5:9; James 3:18). And with all the merrymaking and the spirit of giving at Christmas, what better time for us is there to spread peace to the rest of the world?

Reflection Questions

- What makes you feel peaceful? Or when are you most at peace?

- How have you seen unity or oneness bring peace?

- In what specific way can you bring peace to someone you know this week?

Family Prayer for Peace

Lord, make us instruments of your peace. Where there is hatred, let us sow love; where there is injury, pardon; where there is discord, union; where there is doubt, faith; where there is despair, hope; where there is darkness, light; where there is sadness, joy. Grant that we may not so much seek to be consoled as to console; to be understood as to understand; to be loved as to love. For it is in giving that we receive; it is in pardoning that we are pardoned; and it is in dying that we are born to eternal life. Let it be so. In Jesus's name, amen.
　　　　　　　　　　　　　　　　　　—Prayer of St. Francis of Assisi

Family Advent Wreath (see page 8): Light the Peace candle.

(continued on next page)

Practicing Peace

This week, have each member of the family choose one of the following activities to practice peace (pick one that is age appropriate!):

- Memorize Psalm 4:8.

- Think of five people you can encourage in a way that brings needed peace into their lives.

- Read through the letter to the Ephesians.

- Find an example of someone in the news or on social media bringing peace to others.

- Read or sing the original six stanzas written for the hymn "Silent Night" (StilleNacht.at/en/text-and-music) and reflect on the gift of peace we receive through Christ.

- Read Matthew 5.

- Memorize Matthew 5:1–12.

Peace and Goodwill to You

---------------------------- ◆ ----------------------------

Instead of adding another game or activity idea to
what is undoubtedly a very full Christmas schedule,
here are some ways you can introduce the gift
of peace and rest into your holiday season while
also encouraging a spirit of family togetherness
and enjoying all those decorations you worked
so hard to put up.

Create a peaceful space by the fireplace or Christmas tree or in another cozy space in your home by lighting candles, turning on soothing background music, setting out some treats, brewing hot cocoa, or piling up blankets. Then invite all your family members to come and relax in a way that best suits them, whether that's with a book, crossword, jigsaw puzzle, craft, or even a phone. Feel free to do something together like a puzzle or a read-aloud, but be open to letting everyone choose their own space or use of time (especially the introverts!). The goal is just to be—to wind down after a busy day and to share with your family in the gift of slowing down and experiencing renewal in a season that can feel hurried.

As you discover your family's rhythms over the holidays, write down some other ways you've discovered to rest, recharge, and be together as a family.

-
-
-
-
-
-
-

Decorating Tips for a Peaceful Christmas

Christmas may be the most wonderful time of the year; but with all the holiday shopping, baking, decorating, and hosting, it can also be one of the busiest and most stressful. So how can your family practice peace when there's so much to do? Check out the list on the next page for some ideas on how you can slow down and savor the peace of the season!

Decorating Tips

- If you don't have time to bake, give yourself a break and pick up premade cookies, brownies, a cake, or a pie from the grocery store. Grab a few toppings such as candy, sprinkles, or canned frosting, and have a mini-decorating party with the kids when you get home. Even without spending hours in the kitchen, you can make fun memories and end up with some unique treats!

- If you're not much of a baker at all, don't stress! The holidays are a great time to support local bakeries or friends who are aspiring culinary artists.

- Store each room's Christmas decorations in color-coded or clearly marked bins so you can pull them out one by one and decorate each room separately instead of trying to tackle everything at once. To reduce clutter, place year-round display items in the empty Christmas storage boxes so you can easily switch them back at the end of the holidays.

- Instead of trying to completely deck out every inch of space, allow one item or area in each room to be the main décor feature.

Continue the list from the previous page by using this space to record other time-saving tips and tricks you and your family have come across or created through the years.

-
-
-
-
-
-
-
-
-

Christmas Around the World Fun Facts

More than 160 countries around the world celebrate Christmas with their own unique traditions.

In Bethlehem's Church of St. Alexandria, many Christian groups gather to celebrate evening services in multiple languages.

Because December is actually a summer month in some countries, including Australia, many people celebrate Christmas by having a party on the beach!

In Colombia, the Christmas season begins on December 7 with the Day of the Little Candles.[7]

In Greece, not only trees are decorated with lights, but boats, too!

In Ghana, Christmas Eve is celebrated with songs, dancing, and drumming—sometimes for the entire night![9]

In England, children hang their stockings at the foot of their beds. The celebrations continue through December 26, Boxing Day, when families and friends exchange gifts.[8]

In India, people decorate mango or banana trees instead of evergreens, and Christians will often place lights on their roofs as a symbol that Jesus is the light of the world.

In Ethiopia, Christmas, known as Ganna or Genna, is celebrated on January 7 with a candlelit procession around the church, followed by singing, playing games, and sharing a meal together.

In Japan, one popular Christmas tradition is to eat KFC at some point during the holiday. People even make reservations because it gets so crowded![11]

In the Philippines, Christmas is celebrated with a festival of lanterns, using star-shaped "parol" ornaments.[12]

In Iceland, one favorite national tradition is *Jolabokaflod*, or the "Christmas book flood." Friends and family gift one another books on Christmas Eve, and many people spend all night reading.[10]

In Ukraine, Christmas Eve is marked by a twelve-course, meatless dinner, with each course representing one of the twelve disciples.

In Mexico and other countries with large Catholic populations, many people attend midnight Mass on Christmas Eve. Additional Mexican traditions for the Nochebuena celebration on Christmas Eve include singing, sharing meals together, and breaking a piñata.

In Sweden, many families organize candlelit processions to celebrate St. Lucia's Day, a holiday honoring one of the first female Christian martyrs. Girls dress up as St. Lucia, wearing white dresses and candle wreaths, and serve "S" buns with coffee and mulled wine.

Ingredients

DOUGH

1½ tablespoons yeast

2⅔ cups warm water

⅓ cup granulated sugar

¼ cup unsalted butter, melted

4½ tablespoons honey

4¾ teaspoons salt

6¼ cups all-purpose flour (or flour substitute), plus more for rolling

CARAMEL SAUCE

2 cups brown sugar or coconut sugar

1 cup unsalted butter, cut into pieces

¼ cup corn syrup

¼ cup milk of choice or whipping cream

FILLING

¼ cup unsalted butter, softened

⅔ cup brown sugar

1½ teaspoons ground cinnamon

Directions

- In a large bowl, dissolve the yeast in warm water; stir in the sugar. Set aside until the mixture begins to foam. Add the butter, honey, and salt, then 3 cups of the flour; mix until well blended. Slowly add the remaining flour just until mixture pulls away from the bottom of the bowl. (Dough will be slightly sticky.) Cover with plastic wrap; let rise until doubled (usually between 1 and 2 hours). Punch the dough down; cover and let rise again until doubled.

- While the dough rises, make the caramel sauce: In a medium saucepan over medium heat, heat the brown sugar and butter until melted, stirring occasionally. Remove from the heat; stir in the corn syrup and milk. Pour into two 13x9x2-inch baking pans.

- On a floured surface, roll the dough into a 22x15-inch rectangle. Spread the softened butter over the dough; sprinkle with the brown sugar and cinnamon. Roll up into a log, starting from a long side. Cut into 1¼-inch-wide slices. Gently place each roll, cut side down, in the caramel sauce. Cover the pans with plastic wrap; let rise until doubled (approximately 30 to 60 minutes).

- Bake at 375°F for 25 to 30 minutes or until nicely browned on top. Cool for 1 minute; invert onto a wire rack covered with parchment paper.

Living in Peace

Peace for You

As we are all no doubt aware, the idea of peace during the Christmas season can sometimes sound like a joke. But it doesn't have to be. Peace is a gift that has been given to all of us, if only we will choose to take it. This week, think of what brings you peace and try to set aside time to rest in it. Even if you have only two free minutes in the morning or evening, allow yourself to pause, breathe deeply, and dwell on Jesus's words: "Peace I leave with you; my peace I give you." If you have more time, maybe try reading a book, experimenting with a new recipe, taking a nap, or going on a walk.

Peace for Your Family

Peace is more than stillness or quietness. It's also about having a deep sense of security in knowing that you belong—or rather, knowing who you belong to. As a family, people know you belong to one another because you share blood, genetics, or the same last name, but as a Christian family, you also belong to one another because you belong to Christ. Spend time this week discussing the things that connect and unify you as a family. Create space for each member of your family to share when they have not felt like they belonged and usher in peace among you by seeking each other's forgiveness. Create a list of ways you can reset and be at peace with one another—not just at Christmas, but all year round.

Peace for Your Community

As Christians we are called to be instruments of God's peace. We have been made whole and have a oneness with God because of Christ, and it is our responsibility to share that peace with others! Take some time to pray this week for the global church, for communities suffering from war and poverty, and for those who don't know Jesus as their savior. If that is already a regular part of your prayer life, try thinking of a friend, family member, or neighbor you have had conflict with recently. Commit to being an instrument of God's peace by buying them a gift, taking them some baked goods, shoveling the snow off their driveway, or performing some other action that extends an olive branch and allows them to know you wish them goodwill this season.

Our Traditions

Celebrating the Legacy and Creating the New

Whether passing down beloved and time-tested favorites or coming up with new traditions to share for years to come, use the following pages to record your family's special and unique traditions surrounding the Christmas season.

- _____
  _____
  _____

- _____
  _____
  _____

- _____
  _____
  _____

- _____
  _____
  _____

-

-

-

-

-

-
-
-
-

- _____
  _____
  _____

- _____
  _____
  _____

- _____
  _____
  _____

- _____
  _____
  _____

- _____
  _____
  _____

Christmases Past
Making Memories from Year to Year

As a family, treat the next several pages as your very own "time capsule" of Christmas memories. In the space provided, jot down each person's favorite gift, memory, or activity from the specific year, or write down any hopes for the new year. Feel free to make one family member the "scribe," or invite everyone to record their own entry for the added bit of fun that comes from seeing handwriting styles change from year to year. As you return to this book every Christmas season, these pages will become a true treasure trove of memories to reflect on, laugh about, and share for years to come.

20 _____ _____

_____

_____

_____

_____

20 _____ _____

_____

_____

_____

_____

20 _____ _____

_____

_____

_____

_____

20 _____ _____

_____

_____

_____

_____

20 _____ _____

_____

_____

_____

_____

20 _____ _____

_____

_____

_____

_____

20 _____ _____

_____

_____

_____

_____

20 _____ _____

_____

_____

_____

_____

20 _____ _____

_____

_____

_____

_____

20 _____ _____

_____

_____

_____

_____

20 _____ _____

_____

_____

_____

_____

20 _____ _____

_____

_____

_____

_____

20 _____ _____

_____

_____

_____

_____

20 _____ _____

_____

_____

_____

_____

20 _____ _____

_____

_____

_____

_____

20 _____ _____

_____

_____

_____

_____

20 _____ _____

_____

_____

_____

_____

20 _____ _____

_____

_____

_____

_____

20 _____ _____

_____

_____

_____

_____

20 _____ _____

_____

_____

_____

_____

20 _____ _____

_____

_____

_____

_____

20 _____ _____

_____

_____

_____

_____

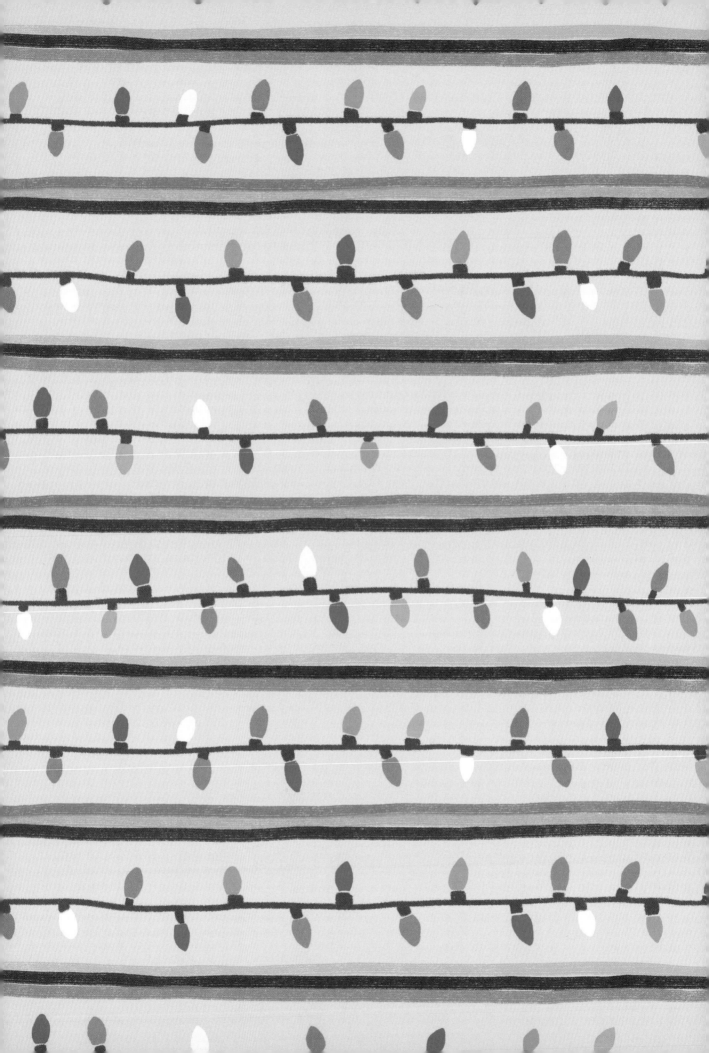

References

[1] Rachel Nuwer, "The First Nativity Scene Was Created in 1223," *Smithsonian Magazine*, December 14, 2012, smithsonianmag.com/smart-news/the-first-nativity-scene-was-created-in-1223-161485505.

[2] "Bethlehem Facts for Kids," Kiddle.co, July 22, 2022, Kids.Kiddle.co/Bethlehem.

[3] Rachel Boulos, "13 Mind-Blowing Facts About Jesus' Birth You Might Not Know," *Live Well. Worry Less.* December 23, 2017, livewellworryless.com/2017/12/23/13-mind-blowing-facts-about-jesus-birth-you-might-not-know.

[4] Rachel Boulos, "13 Mind-Blowing Facts About Jesus' Birth You Might Not Know," *Live Well. Worry Less.* December 23, 2017, livewellworryless.com/2017/12/23/13-mind-blowing-facts-about-jesus-birth-you-might-not-know.

[5] "Saint Nicholas Day," kidskonnect.com, kidskonnect.com/religion/saint-nicholas-day.

[6] "Saint Nicholas Day: Fun Facts About St. Nick," "From St. Nicholas to Santa Claus," Medievalists, 2014, medievalists.net/2014/12/st-nicholas-santa-claus/

[7] James Cooper, "Christmas in Colombia," WhyChristmas.com, whychristmas.com/cultures/colombia.

[8] Regina Graff, "Christmas Around the World," Kids World Travel Guide, kids-world-travel-guide.com/christmas-around-the-world.html.

[9] James Cooper, "Christmas in Ghana," WhyChristmas.com, whychristmas.com/cultures/ghana.

[10] Ashley Leath, "Why Icelanders Spend Every Christmas Eve Reading Books and Drinking Cocoa," *Country Living*, November 29, 2021, countryliving.com/life/a46204/jolabokaflod-iceland-christmas-reading-tradition.

[11] "Countries That Celebrate Christmas," World Population Review, worldpopulationreview.com/country-rankings/countries-that-celebrate-christmas.

[12] Andrew Lisa, "How Christmas Is Celebrated Around the World," Stacker.com, November 17, 2021, stacker.com/stories/2214/how-christmas-celebrated-around-world.

'TIS THE SEASON

All Scripture quotations are taken
from the Holy Bible, New International
Version®, NIV®. Copyright © 1973,
1978, 1984, 2011 by Biblica Inc.™ Used
by permission of Zondervan. All rights
reserved worldwide. (www.zondervan.com).
The "NIV" and "New International Version"
are trademarks registered in the United States
Patent and Trademark Office by Biblica Inc.™

ISBN 9-780-593-58047-9

Published in the United States by WaterBrook, an imprint of
Random House, a division of Penguin Random House LLC.

Ink & Willow® and its colophon are registered trademarks
of Penguin Random House LLC.

Printed in China

2023—First Edition

WaterBrookMultnomah.com

10 9 8 7 6 5 4 3 2

SPECIAL SALES Most WaterBrook and Ink & Willow books are available
at special quantity discounts when purchased in bulk by corporations,
organizations, and special-interest groups. Custom imprinting or excerpting
can also be done to fit special needs. For information, please email
specialmarketscms@penguinrandomhouse.com.